EVENTIDE

Barney Norris

EVENTIDE

OBERON BOOKS
LONDON

WWW.OBERONBOOKS.COM

First published in 2015 by Oberon Books Ltd
521 Caledonian Road, London N7 9RH
Tel: +44 (0) 20 7607 3637 / Fax: +44 (0) 20 7607 3629
e-mail: info@oberonbooks.com
www.oberonbooks.com

A catalogue record for this book is available from the British
Library.

PB ISBN: 9781783199112
E ISBN: 9781783199129

Cover image by Charlie Young

Printed, bound and converted
by CPI Group (UK) Ltd, Croydon, CR0 4YY.

For Dad.

With thanks to my friends at the Cricketers in Tangley
and Costa in Salisbury; Alice, Chloe, Ashleigh, Up
In Arms and all the actors who supported the play's
development in the workshops; Leyla, Mehmet, Ben,
Jack, Laura, Charlotte, Miriam and all at the Arcola
Theatre; Lucy, Amy, Sherrell and the North Wall; Arts
Council England; Frank and Elizabeth Brenan; all our
supporters and touring partners; Rozzy Wyatt and Judy
Daish Associates; George Spender and Oberon Books;
Lauren Clancy, Iain Gillie, John McGrath, Frances
Macadam, Peter Tyas and Lucy Williams, our Advisory
Board; Hasan, Paddy, Ellie, James, both the Georges,
Simon, Tammy, Becky, Jennie, Rachael and especially
to Charlie.

UP IN ARMS

Honest, human, affecting, revealing:

we make plays about people and the places they're from.

Up In Arms is an award-winning touring theatre company from the south west of England. The company was founded in 2008 by Alice Hamilton and Barney Norris, who began working together as teenagers in their local youth theatre. We have performed above pubs, in classrooms, hospices, woods and village halls, and in many of the UK's leading theatres.

Our work is built around a permanent ensemble of like-minded theatremakers. Our plays grow out of workshops and conversations over years, and through our Participation programme we work with hundreds of people each year, encouraging them to engage creatively with their lives through making theatre.

KEEP IN TOUCH – JOIN OUR MAILING LIST

www.upinarms.org.uk | director@upinarms.org.uk
Twitter: @upinarmstheatre | Facebook: "Up In Arms"

Supported using public funding by
ARTS COUNCIL ENGLAND
LOTTERY FUNDED

Arcola Theatre is one of London's leading off-West End theatres.

arcola theatre

Locally engaged and internationally minded, Arcola stages a diverse programme of plays, operas and musicals. World-class productions from major artists appear alongside cutting-edge work from the most exciting emerging companies.

Arcola delivers one of London's most extensive community engagement programmes, creating over 5000 opportunities every year. By providing research and development space to diverse artists, Arcola champions theatre that's more engaging and representative. Its pioneering environmental initiatives are internationally renowned, and aim to make Arcola the world's first carbon-neutral theatre.

With grateful thanks to our ushers, interns, volunteers and those on work placements, and to our Supporters, Patrons and other donors.

 Supported using public funding by **ARTS COUNCIL ENGLAND** LOTTERY FUNDED

 Esmée Fairbairn FOUNDATION

J PAUL GETTY JNR CHARITABLE TRUST

Bloomberg

⊬ Hackney

www.arcolatheatre.com   020 7503 1646   24 Ashwin Street, Dalston, London E8 3DL

EVENTIDE 2015 TOUR DATES

23rd September – 17th October
ARCOLA THEATRE
arcolatheatre.com | 020 7503 1646

22nd – 24th October
THEATRE ROYAL BURY ST EDMUNDS
theatreroyal.org | 01284 755127

28th – 31st October
THE NORTH WALL, OXFORD
thenorthwall.com | 01865 319450

3rd – 7th November
SALISBURY PLAYHOUSE
salisburyplayhouse.com | 01722 320117

10th – 14th November
BRISTOL TOBACCO FACTORY
tobaccofactorytheatres.com | 0117 902 0344

OUR SUPPORTERS

This play was made possible by our Supporters, a group of people who believe in the importance of the stories we tell and the way we tell them. We would like to thank everyone whose engagement and enthusiasm gets our shows onstage.

VERY SPECIAL THANKS

Frank and Elizabeth Brenan, Alison Lowdon, David Owen Norris, Sarah, Pete and Ruth Shepherd, Peter and Jane Hamilton.

SPECIAL THANKS

Offline Magazine, Rachel Bebb, Susanna Bishop, Farhana Bhula, Richard Broyd, John Cox, Veronica Dewan, Bekah Diamond, Hasan Dixon, Esther Ruth Elliott, John Foster, Victoria Gee, Hannah Groombridge, Anna Hamilton and Angus Meryon, Juliette Kelly-Fleming, Suzy McClintock, Alice Malin, Linda Morse, Janet Rieder, Stephanie Ressort, Celia Swan.

THANKS

The Workers Educational Association, Lindsay Balkwell, Sarah Blake, John Burgess, Milly Ellis, Fiona, Rob and Poppy Evans, Aidan Grounds, Barbara Houseman, Luke Holbrook, Katharine Ingle, Max Lindsay, Alex Orchard-Lisle, Naomi Petersen, Ivan Richardson, Ilara Rocchi, Kandy Rohmann, George Warren.

JOIN US

To join the Supporters Scheme, access exclusive opportunities and become part of our work, visit **upinarms.org.uk.**

COMPANY BIOGRAPHIES

Chloe Courtney | Producer
Chloe has produced all of Up In Arms' work since 2013. She is
the Project Manager for the National Alliance for Arts in Criminal
Justice and was previously Project Co-ordinator at Complicite. She
has produced work for Southwark Playhouse, Oxford Playhouse,
BAC, Wilderness Festival, Secret Garden Party, Shunt Vaults and
Liverpool's City of Culture Festival. This year she was awarded a
Stage One producer bursary.

Rebecca Denby | Assistant Stage Manager
With Up In Arms: *Visitors.*
Theatre includes: *Broadway Showtunes* (Bournemouth Pavilion);
Lardo (Old Red Lion); *The Russian Doctor* (Birmingham Rep); *The
Horror The Horror – The Final Curtain* (Wilton's Music Hall).

George Dennis | Sound Designer
With Up In Arms: *Visitors.*
At Arcola: *peddling* (also 59E59, New York/High Tide Festival)
Theatre includes: *Primetime, Fireworks, Liberian Girl* (Royal
Court); *Brave New World, Regeneration* (Royal and Derngate/Touring
Consortium); *Harrogate* (High Tide Festival); *Chicken* (Eastern Angles/
Unity Theatre); *Image of an Unknown Young Woman, Eclipsed, The Edge
of our Bodies, Dances of Death* (Gate Theatre); *Beautiful Thing* (Arts
Theatre/UK Tour); *A Breakfast of Eels, The Last Yankee* (Print Room);
Mametz (National Theatre of Wales); *Minotaur* (Polka Theatre/Clwyd
Theatr Cymru); *Spring Awakening* (Headlong); *The Island* (Young Vic);
Love Your Soldiers (Sheffield Crucible Studio); *Thark* (Park Theatre);
Moth (Bush Theatre/HighTide Festival); *Hello/Goodbye* (Hampstead
Theatre); *Liar Liar* (Unicorn Theatre); *Good Grief* (Theatre Royal
Bath/UK Tour); *The Seven Year Itch* (Salisbury Playhouse); *When Did
You Last See My Mother?* (Trafalgar Studios); *The Living Room* (Jermyn
Street Theatre); *Debris, The Seagull, The Only True History of Lizzie
Finn* (Southwark Playhouse); *A Life, Foxfinder* (Finborough Theatre).

Hasan Dixon | Mark
With Up In Arms: *Fear Of Music.*
At Arcola: *The Spanish Tragedy.*
Theatre includes: *War Horse* (National Theatre); *The Alchemist* (Liverpool Playhouse); *The Glass Menagerie* (Everyman Cheltenham); *You: the Player* (West Yorkshire Playhouse); *Yerma* (Gate); *Ghosts* (Hull Truck); *The Return* (Southwark Playhouse); *None But Friends* (Rose Theatre Kingston); *The Little Prince* (Exeter Bike Shed).
TV: *Call The Midwife, Silent Witness, A Touch of Frost, Doctors.*
Film: *This Is Not Happening, John Carter, Coincidence.*

James Doherty | John
Theatre includes: *London Road, NT:50* (National Theatre); *Chicago, Les Miserables, A Slice of Saturday Night* (West End); *Kiss Me Kate* (Royal Albert Hall); *God of Carnage* (Northampton Theatre Royal); *Teenage Kicks* (Assembly Rooms); *Teechers* (Haymarket); *House and Garden* (Harrogate Theatre); *Gangster No. 1, Harlequinade, Separate Tables* (King's Head); *Joey 'n' Gina's Wedding* (Cafe Royal); *Saucy Jack* (Queen's Theatre); *Buddy* (UK and Toronto); *The Rocky Horror Show* (UK tour).
TV: *From the Cradle to the Grave, The Job Lot, Top Coppers, Him and Her The Wedding, Veep, Endeavour, Ambassadors, Boomers, The IT Crowd, Phoneshop, Count Arthur Strong, Coronation Street, Waterloo Road, Watson and Oliver, The Royal Bodyguard, A Touch of Cloth, Miranda, Rev, Mongrels, The Thick of It, Katy Brand's Big Ass Show, The Increasingly Poor Decisions of Todd Margaret, Footballer's Wives, Small Potatoes, Is Harry On The Boat?, Night and Day, Hotel Getaway, Eastenders, Casualty, All About George, According to Bex, Holby City, Doctors, The Royal, Peak Practice, The Jury, The Wyvern Mystery, Bob Martin, Family Affairs, Dad, 2 Point 4 Children, In Sickness and In Health, Hippies, The Bill.*
Film: *London Road, In The Loop, Closed Circuit, Deviation, The Forgotten, Inbred, Verity's Summer, City Rats, Backbeat.*

Alice Hamilton | Director
Alice is the co-Artistic Director of Up In Arms. Direction for the company includes *Visitors* (Arcola, Bush Theatre and tour), *Fear Of Music* (tour with Out of Joint) and *At First Sight* (tour and Latitude Festival). Other work includes *Orson's Shadow* (Southwark Playhouse), *15 16 17* (Old Vic New Voices), *Belarus* (Arcola for the Miniaturists), *Extinct* and *Starcrossed* (Bush for Courting Drama) and *The Kingdom of Me* (Park Theatre for Hatch). As Staff Director: *Man and Superman* (National Theatre).

Rachael Harrison | Marketing and Producing Assistant
Rachael is an actress and voiceover artist who has toured nationally with Another Midas theatre and performed internationally as an independent cabaret performer. Other theatre includes *Love's Labour's Lost, Henry V, A Midsummer Night's Dream* (Theatre Royal Winchester) and *A Midsummer Night's Dream* (Windsor Globe). Rachael currently works at the Arcola Theatre on the front of house team and is beginning to work as a theatre producer.

George Nichols | Assistant Director
George has just graduated from Bristol, where he read Drama. Theatre includes *Oddity* (Edinburgh Festival), *Here* (rehearsed reading, Bristol Old Vic), *The Allotment* (Alma Tavern), *Entertaining Mr. Sloane* and *Zoo Story*. He was a researcher for *The Absence of War* (Headlong).

Barney Norris | Writer
Barney is the co-Artistic Director of Up In Arms. He won the Critics' Circle Award and the Offwestend Award for Most Promising Playwright for *Visitors*. His short plays, collected as *What You Wish For In Youth*, are published by Oberon. His book *To Bodies Gone: The Theatre of Peter Gill* is published by Seren. His first novel, *Five Rivers Met On A Wooded Plain*, will be published by Doubleday in 2016. He is the Martin Esslin Playwright in Residence at Keble College, Oxford.

James Perkins | Designer
Theatre includes: *The Gathered Leaves* (Park Theatre); *Little Shop of Horrors* (Royal Exchange, Manchester); *Breeders* (St James Theatre); *Shiver, Lost In Yonkers* (Watford Palace Theatre); *Ciphers* (Bush Theatre/Out Of Joint); *1001 Nights* (Unicorn Theatre/Transport Theatre); *Liar Liar* (Unicorn Theatre); *Girl In The Yellow Dress* (Salisbury Playhouse); *Microcosm* (Soho Theatre); *Dances Of Death* (Gate Theatre); *The Fantasist's Waltz* (York Theatre Royal); *Stockwell* (Tricycle Theatre); *Carthage, Foxfinder, The Bofors Gun, Trying* (Finborough Theatre); *The Only True History Of Lizzie Finn, Floyd Collins* (Southwark Playhouse); *The Marriage Of Figaro* (Wilton's Music Hall); *The Life Of Stuff, Desolate Heaven, Threads, Many Moons* (Theatre503); *The Hotel Plays* (Grange Hotel); *St John's Night, Saraband* (Jermyn Street Theatre); *Pirates, HMS Pinafore* (Buxton Opera House); *Matters of Life And Death* (Contemporary Dance UK Tour);

Iolanthe, The Way Through The Woods (Pleasance Theatre, London); *The Faerie Queene* (Lilian Baylis, Sadler's Wells); *The Wonder* (BAC). James created Story Whores. He is an associate of Forward Theatre Project and one third of paper/scissors/stone.

Ellie Piercy | Liz
Theatre includes: *The Heresy of Love, As You Like It, Blue Stockings, All's Well That Ends Well, The Merry Wives of Windsor, Liberty, Romeo and Juliet* (Shakespeare's Globe); *The Widowing of Mrs Holroyd* (Orange Tree); *Much Ado About Nothing* (Manchester Royal Exchange); *Taming the Tempest, A Touch of the Sun* (Salisbury Playhouse); *How To Be A Giant, The Eyes of Marie, The Best In Town* (Unicorn); *Plunder* (Watermill).
TV: *Doctors, The World of the Impressionists.*
Film: *Brothers of War, Mr Duncan.*

Jennie Quirk | Costume Supervisor
Theatre includes: Assistant Wardrobe Supervisor – *An Inspector Calls* (PW Productions); Wardrobe Mistress – *Blue Stockings, Metamorphosis* (West Glamorgan Youth Theatre); Wardrobe Mistress – *Beautiful Thing* (Curve Theatre/Nottingham Playhouse); Wardrobe Supervisor – *Ruddigore* (Charles Court Opera Company); Wardrobe Supervisor/ Mistress – *Bad Jews, Accolade, Breeders* (St James Theatre); Costume Designer/Supervisor – *Man's Ambition* (West Glamorgan Theatre); Stylist – Joe Stilgoe photoshoot; Wardrobe assistant – *The Drowned Man* (Punchdrunk); Wardrobe Assistant – Robbie Williams live, *Swings Both Ways* (Palladium); Dresser – *The Curious Incident of the Dog in the Night Time* (National Theatre Productions); Costume maker – *Grim Tales* (West Glamorgan Youth Theatre); Costume Maker – *Love Sick* (All In Theatre Company); Wardrobe Assistant – *Bingo* (The Young Vic).

Tamsin Rose | Production Manager
At Arcola: *Clarion, Shrapnel: 34 Fragments of a Massacre, Happy Endings, Eldorado.*
Theatre includes: *The Lone Pine Club* (Pentabus); *Three Tales Opera* (IMAX); *Lady Anna, Toast* (Park Theatre); *Dead Simple, Perfect Murder* (JASS Productions); *King Lear, The Canterbury Tales* (Guildford Shakespeare Company); *My Mother Said I Never Should, Mother Goose* (The Theatre Chipping Norton); *Brundibar* (Mahogany Opera); *The Little Green Swallow* (Peacock Theatre); *Last Days of Limehouse*

(Limehouse Town Hall); *Donkey Heart* (Old Red Lion & Trafalgar Studios); *AtoZ of Mrs. P* (Southwark Playhouse); *Evita* (European tour); *Black Coffee, Aladdin, Witness for the Prosecution, Murder on Air, Grass is Greener, Pack of Lies* (Theatre Royal Windsor and tour); *Chin Chin, Fallen Angels, Laughter in the Rain, A Daughter's A Daughter, Dreamboats and Petticoats, Whistle Down the Wind* (Bill Kenwright Ltd); *Eugenie Grande* (Assembly Rooms); *Woody Sez* (UK Arts); *Cinderella* (Grimaldi Forum Monaco).

Simon Gethin Thomas | Lighting Designer
With Up In Arms: *Visitors, Fear Of Music.*
Theatre includes: *Rhythm of Silence* (Theatre Royal Bath); *Rent* (Birmingham Hippodrome Patrick Centre); *Eye of a Needle* (Southwark Playhouse); *Sweeney Todd* (Twickenham Theatre); *Pincher Martin* (Britten Theatre); *Gone Viral, I Cinna* (St James Theatre); the Arensky Chamber Orchestra (Queen Elizabeth Hall, South Bank Centre).
Simon is a Visiting Tutor for Technical Theatre to the St Ives Theatre, Cornwall.

Charlie Young | Company Stage Manager
Charlie has been the Company Stage Manager for all Up In Arms' work since 2013.
At Arcola: *Visitors, Between Us.*
Theatre includes: *The Tiger Who Came to Tea* (Nick Brooke Productions); *Garden* (Pleasance Courtyard); *The Snail and The Whale, Emily Brown and the Thing, The Snow Dragon* (Tall Stories); *Miss Caledonia* (House); *Barbican Box* (Barbican); *Amazon Beaming* workshop (Complicite); *Hag, The Girl With The Iron Claws* (The Wrong Crowd); *Idylls of the King* (Oxford Playhouse); *Pinocchio* (Berry Theatre); *Jesus Christ Superstar* (Ljubljana Festival, Slovenia); *The Hairy Ape, Antigone* (Southwark Playhouse); *Third Floor* (Trafalgar Studios); *Much Ado About Nothing, Twelfth Night* (Ludlow Festival).

Coming soon: the debut novel by Barney Norris

FIVE RIVERS MET ON A WOODED PLAIN

'There exists in all of us a song waiting to be sung which is as heart-stopping and vertiginous as the peak of the cathedral. That is the meaning of this quiet city, where the spire soars into the blue, where rivers and stories weave into one another, where lives intertwine.'

The peace of an evening in Salisbury is shattered by a car crash, and five lives collide. A flower seller, a schoolboy, a farmer, an army wife, a security guard, all facing their own personal disasters, all connect for a moment in the shadow of this accident. As one of those lives hangs in the balance, the stories of all five unfold, drawn together by collision and coincidence into a web of love, grief and hope mapping the small joys and everyday tragedies of life in England now.

Doubleday

Published on 21st April 2016

Pre-order your copy at **Waterstones.com**

Eventide was first presented by Up In Arms and Arcola Theatre in association with the North Wall on September 25th, 2015, with the following company:

Hasan Dixon – MARK
James Doherty – JOHN
Ellie Piercy – LIZ

Director, Alice Hamilton
Designer, James Perkins
Lighting Designer, Simon Gethin Thomas
Sound Designer, George Dennis
Production Manager, Tamsin Rose
Company Stage Manager, Charlie Young
Assistant Stage Manager, Rebecca Denby
Costume Supervisor, Jennie Quirk
Producer, Chloe Courtney
Assistant Director, George Nichols
Marketing and Producing Assistant, Rachael Harrison

This text went to press before the end of rehearsals so may differ from the final performance.

Characters

JOHN

a pub landlord

MARK

a young man

LIZ

a village organist

You're pretending this isn't your life. You think it's going to happen some other time. When you're dead you'll realise you were alive now.

Caryl Churchill, *Mad Forest*

ONE

MARK is sitting with a toolkit. Enter JOHN, pushing a wheelbarrow.

JOHN: Bloke walks into a pub. And he goes to the bar and
orders a pint and while he's waiting for it this feller sidles
up to him and says do you wanna buy a ferret? Scuse
me? Our hero replies. Do you wanna buy a ferret? The
feller says again. Not really says our man. Ah, but this is
no ordinary ferret, says the other feller. No no no. This
ferret gives the best blow job in the world. You what? Says
the first bloke. I'm telling you, says the stranger, I am in
possession of a ferret that gives the best blow job in the
world. However, it's coming up Christmas and I've got a
tax bill to pay, so I need to realise some of my assets, and
for that reason I'm willing to let you have this ferret for the
ever so reasonable sum of five hundred quid. A monkey
for a ferret? Asks the first bloke. Monkey's five hundred
quid, Mark, in case you're not as down with the kids as I
am. Case you're not street. Where was I? Tell you what,
says the other feller, don't just take my word for it. I can
see you're the sort of bloke likes to know what he's buying,
fair enough. I respect that. I admire it. So why not pop in
the gents and give him a test run? And he slips this ferret in
the other feller's pocket, and the other feller's not sure what
to do so rather than give it back and risk offence, he goes
off to the gents. He's English, see, he doesn't want to say
no directly. So he goes in this cubicle, and he's alone with
this ferret, and he thinks, this has got to be a practical joke.
There's no way I'm letting my cock anywhere near this
ferret's teeth. But he's in the cubicle now. He'll feel like an
idiot if he comes out without having tried it. And he thinks
to himself, wouldn't it be amazing if it was true? Wouldn't
it be an amazing thing if there was a ferret who gave the
best blow job in the world? And isn't that worth a little
risk, a thought like that? So he takes a deep breath, and
opens his flies, and five minutes later he's back in the bar
with a grin a mile wide saying he has to get to a cash point.
So he buys this ferret, and takes it home, and he shows it to

his wife. I've bought a ferret, he says. Why? Says the wife. Well this is no ordinary ferret, he says. This ferret gives the best blow job in the world. That's wonderful, says his wife, but what do you want me to do with it? Easy, he says. Teach it to cook and fuck off.

MARK laughs.

MARK: That's good that is, I like that.

JOHN: Mm.

MARK: It's got a twist at the –

JOHN: Jokes don't want deconstructing, Mark, it spoils 'em. Let it remain as a beautiful snowflake.

MARK: Right. Yeah.

JOHN starts to fill the wheelbarrow with firewood.

MARK: Stocking up?

JOHN: Mm.

MARK: Hot day for a fire.

JOHN: Blaze in my grate every day of the year. It's part of what people come for, you know?

MARK: Oh yeah.

JOHN: Horrible mangy dogs and an unpleasantly hot public bar. That's what I'm selling really. More than the ham egg and chips. All kinds of places shift food and drink, it's sweat and dogs make me distinctive. I'd be down on couples booking dirty weekends if I didn't have a flickering log fire to offer them, and the infidelity trade's big business. People having affairs tip well out of guilt.

MARK: Fair enough.

JOHN: She meant a lot to you didn't she.

MARK: Not – yeah. She did, yeah.

JOHN: I suppose it's not my place.

MARK: You're all right.

JOHN: Guess you're getting it from everyone.

MARK: Not every one's got as big a mouth as you.

JOHN: That's my job, isn't it. Ask all the awkward questions. Listen to all the awkward answers. Know all the secrets. That's the art. Innit. Sometimes all your life feels like a falling away of everything from you, don't you think? I think that. And when you get to considering it, it's hard to see the point really, innit. Where was I? You have to carry on though.

MARK: No 'have to' about it, far as I see.

JOHN: Mm?

MARK: Time just keeps fuckin' happenin' to you, don't it. 'Have to' makes it sound like there's a – I dunno, like there's a choice. It's more like – it's like you're on a Megabus, right, or maybe a National Express, I dunno, and you pass a crash on the other side of the motorway, and you want to have a look, you know? But before you can get a proper goosey you're past it, and the road's going on, and you're hurried away from the scene of the accident. Like. Yeah. Because you're headed for Plymouth or wherever, you weren't meant to stop there. That's what absolutely everything is like. Fuck it, anyway. How are you John, are you all right? It's not a great day for you either is it.

JOHN: Today?

MARK: What with –

JOHN: I know what you're saying. It's not great, no.

MARK: What will you do, do you think?

JOHN: I don't know. Sit perfectly still. Don't have the energy for anything except a drink.

MARK: It's not good, man.

JOHN: Not in the long run, no, but I get a certain bitter pleasure from it now. And I don't know what's so wrong with sitting perfectly still. When Chris Marsden announced he was going to retire – you remember Chris Marsden, used to play centre mid for Southampton? – he went on the radio and said his plan was to go to a beach in Greece and just sit there. In the sun. And the interviewer asked him, joking like, don't you think you'll get bored? He just laughed, he said no mate, I think I'll get tanned.

MARK laughs.

JOHN: You ever read W.H.Davies?

MARK: Don't think so.

JOHN: He was a tramp. And a poet. For a little while he lived in a shed at the bottom of Edward Thomas's garden. Who was a manic depressive. And also a poet, who died in the war. Which is one of the best comedies never written. Not the war, the two poets. And W.H.Davies wrote this poem, 'a poor life this if, full of care, we have no time to stand and stare'. You know that?

MARK: *Four Weddings and a Funeral.*

JOHN: It was the Centre Parcs advert actually, but never mind. What I'm saying is, W.H.Davies, when he was living in Edward Thomas's shed, he wasn't a million miles from here. All in the shadow of the Forest. Same as Chrissy Marsden, see? And I don't think people recognise that there's a distinctive outlook which belongs to this part of the world, which is about sitting around doing fuck all for as long as you possibly can. That's what it's all about isn't it, pubs and cricket or whatever. Sitting around doing nothing. And people associate that with laziness, but it's not. It's the embodiment of a – of a philosophy.

MARK: What?

John: They toil not, neither do they spin.

Mark: What?

John: Bible, innit. You know that one don't you? Bible's full of stuff about not having to work. Parable of the prodigal son's all about that. Fucking, don't worry about putting a shift in, fuck off on a jolly and we'll do you a roast.

Mark: Yeah, I never get that one.

John: Why?

MARK: I don't know why people give more credit to the bloke who fucked off and cocked up then came home than the bloke who stuck around and got on with things.

JOHN: I think it's about getting converts.

MARK: How?

JOHN: Well it was a new religion wasn't it. Christianity. So it was like a message to say, be nice to floating voters. They'll end up deciding the election.

MARK: Right.

JOHN: Or something else.

MARK: What?

JOHN: Well I was just thinking, maybe it's a way of saying, try and do something with your life. Be deliberate, you know? During your life, try and make one conscious decision. Cos you'll always have where you came from. So you might as well have a go at trying to find something else for as long as you've got a home to come back to, and not just truck along the same furrow for ever.

MARK: It'll all get better, you know, John.

JOHN: It might get number. I'll give you that. But it'll always have happened, and nothing that's happened to you, really happened to you like that ever gets better, does it. It might get number, I'll give you that. Look at me. I ought to be comforting you.

MARK: No –

JOHN: You did care for her, didn't you.

MARK: It's strange. Cos I did, I can admit that now, I did. Yeah. And I feel – but I've no more right to grieve than anyone else, have I. Cos. No reason to feel any – more than anyone else. We were close for a while, at school or whatever, yeah, and I loved all that, when we were at school, but not for any real reason, only because we shared a few classes, you know? And I've never had the kind of girlfriend where you're – you know, where you're happy, so I don't know, but I think people who are close like, I mean properly close, like, maybe I mean people who are in love, sort of thing, there must always be more to it than that, mustn't there? Some – feeling you both have, which is more than just sharing a few classes, and you fancying her and her not minding you. Which is more or less. Maybe not for the likes of me, maybe I'll end up taking what I can get or have to stay on my own for ever, or whatever, but for the likes of her, you know? There must be actual love that's like a thing, that exists. So I don't feel more important than anyone else. No. I don't feel I should be, anyway. So it's strange how I'm feeling today.

JOHN: How, strange?

MARK: Because I loved her, to be honest. Yeah. Yeah. I've never said that to anyone before.

JOHN: Not even to her?

MARK: Course not. Fuck. Last of all to her.

JOHN: But you loved her.

MARK: I still do. That doesn't stop, does it.

JOHN: No. It just becomes something you can cope with. Or that's what we must both hope.

MARK: Sometimes I sort of wish I'd never felt anything in my life.

JOHN: I hear that.

MARK: Yeah?

JOHN: Look at us. Do you want a drink?

MARK: I'd better not.

JOHN: Let me stand you a beer. You're earning that today. This is my last day as a landlord, let me stand you a beer.

MARK: Just a bottle, not a pint.

JOHN: All right. I might have one with you.

MARK: Don't you need to start prepping lunch mate?

JOHN: In a bit. There's a little while left.

Enter LIZ.

LIZ: Morning!

JOHN: Hello Liz, you all right?

LIZ: I'm OK, how are you?

JOHN: Wanna hear a joke?

LIZ: Really?

JOHN: Go on, little joke.

LIZ: Go on then.

JOHN: Bloke walks into a pub. And he goes to the bar and orders a pint and while he's waiting this feller sidles up to him and says do you wanna buy a ferret? Scuse me? Our hero replies. Do you wanna buy a ferret? The feller says again. Not really. Ah, but this is no ordinary ferret, says the other feller. This ferret gives the best blow job in the world. You what? Asks the first bloke. I'm telling you, says the stranger, I am in possession of a ferret that gives the best blow job in the world. However, it's coming up for Christmas and I've got a tax bill to pay, so I'm gonna let you have it for the ever so reasonable sum of five hundred quid. Five hundred quid for a ferret? Asks the first bloke. Tell you what, says the other feller, you don't just have to take my word for it. Why not pop in the gents and give the little feller a test run? And he slips this ferret in the other feller's pocket, and the other feller goes off to the gents, and ten minutes later he's back in the bar with a grin a mile wide saying he has to get to a cash point. So he buys this ferret, and takes it home, and he shows it to his wife. I've bought a ferret, he says. Why? Says the wife. Well this is no ordinary ferret, he says. This ferret gives the best blow job in the world. That's wonderful, says his wife, but what do you want me to do with it? Easy, he says. Teach it to cook and fuck off.

MARK laughs again. LIZ doesn't.

LIZ: You're awful, John, you know that?

JOHN: It's a reputation I try to live down to. Lemonade?

LIZ: Yes please.

JOHN: I'll get it.

LIZ: You don't have to –

JOHN: Glad to. Don't worry. Always silver service when you come to The White Horse.

LIZ: Well. Thanks.

Exit JOHN with the wheelbarrow, which is now full of firewood. LIZ lights up.

LIZ: Sorry – do you mind if I smoke?

MARK: Go ahead.

LIZ: This is the smoker's table, isn't it.

MARK: I think you can smoke anywhere outside really, but this is where people come, innit, yeah.

LIZ: Sort of behind the bikeshed I suppose. Behind the woodpile, anyway. And we all started doing it because it felt a bit naughty. Sex sex sex, isn't it.

MARK: What?

LIZ: Smoking. I don't know where sex stops and smoking begins.

MARK: No?

LIZ: Cos you start to become sexualised, don't you. When you're growing up, you start to feel – but you don't realise maybe that that's what's happening. Not straight away. All you know is you want to do something – I don't know, you feel – and there's this ban on tobacco advertising, so that must be naughty, right? So maybe you wanna do that. And James Dean's always smoking, and you just know he's shagged every night, and deep down you know it's about getting laid really, you do know, so they sort of get –

MARK: Linked in your head.

LIZ: That's it! And there's all the – I don't know, there's a sort of phallic aspect isn't there? Look at that. Of course a penis is bigger than that, in most cases, but all the same. Do you want one?

MARK: You're all right.

LIZ: Or maybe it's more about nipples, I don't know. Maybe fags are like, a flight from sexuality, maybe it's wanting to get back to sucking on nipples, while you're growing up, after a ride, so you get something to put in your mouth. And it's not a cock, it's a thumb to suck. But on fire. I'm Liz by the way.

MARK: Oh. Mark.

LIZ: Hi Mark. Sorry, I – mm. Sure you don't want one?

MARK: Actually would you mind?

LIZ: Course not.

MARK: Thanks.

They light up.

LIZ: God, I was gasping. I don't like to smoke in the car. I
volunteer for Contact the Elderly, do you know them?

MARK: Erm –

LIZ: They had some very good adverts about two years ago,
sort of riffing on *When Harry Met Sally*, do you remember
them?

MARK: I don't think so.

LIZ: Anyway, that was how I heard about them. They're
great. Their thing is that older people get very isolated,
very alone, so they arrange these tea parties. And you can
volunteer either to host one where you live or to drive the
elderly people to and from these parties, and stay with
them while they're there to make sure they're all right.

MARK: Nursery school for old people.

LIZ: Yeah, I suppose. Anyway, I live in a shoe box so I can't
have people round, but I can drive, so I volunteer for that
bit, which I love. But the trouble is it means I don't like
to smoke in my car, or it stinks of fags and I worry they'll
think I'm degenerate, or choke to death on second hand
smoke. So whenever I get to the end of a drive I'm always
gasping.

MARK: Right.

LIZ: You don't smoke usually?

MARK: No. I always thought I'd smoke when I grew up, cos
my Dad did –

LIZ: Then it killed him?!

MARK: It did actually, yeah.

LIZ: Oh God I'm so sorry.

MARK: No, but it wasn't that that stopped me.

LIZ: No?

MARK: It was the smoking ban, really. You know? Cos my idea
of smoking couldn't actually come true, like, by the time
I started earning enough money to buy any fags. So there
didn't seem much point in it. Yeah. There you go, that's
how it goes, isn't it.

LIZ: Little bit of your cultural inheritance robbed from you.

MARK: Yeah.

LIZ: Is it true they're putting the war memorial back up today?

MARK: What?

LIZ: Well I'm playing for this funeral this morning. I'm the
organist for the church, you see. And this funeral, it's
this girl from round here who drove her car into the war
memorial and died last week. So sad. She was back from
university and driving too fast, and apparently she didn't
have her car with her in London so she hadn't been driving
for a few months and she was out of practise and she sort
of lost control. It's so sad isn't it. I don't think they should
let such young people on the roads, they can't be trusted.
It's a wonder she didn't hurt anyone else. But anyway, the
vicar told me when I was parking my car, I always park
my car there first then have my fag here and a lemonade to
spruce up because I don't like smoking near the church in
case Jesus sees me, the vicar said there's actually going to
be work being done on the war memorial today, while the
bloody hearse goes by! They'll be putting it back together
while she gets driven past, how tasteless is that?

MARK: Right.

LIZ: Did you know her, the girl who died? Are you from round
here at all?

Enter JOHN with three drinks.

JOHN: An Englishman, an Irishman, a Scotsman, a Dutchman, a Belgian, a Welsh bloke, a Frenchman, a German, a Spaniard, an Uruguayan, a Brazilian, an American, a Canadian mounted policeman, an Indian, an Australian, a Kiwi, a Peruvian, a Slovenian, a Russian, an Ukrainian and a Chinaman walk up to a nightclub, and the doorman says sorry gents, you can't come in. Why not? They all ask. The doorman shrugs. Because you haven't got a Thai. Thank God for Holsten Pils.

MARK: Cheers.

LIZ: That was actually much less racist than I expected it to be, John, well done. You can keep that one.

JOHN: No, they're like mayflies, jokes. I keep 'em for one day only. After that they're yours to cherish and disseminate or otherwise discard.

LIZ: Well I obviously never tell any of them to anyone I know.

JOHN: Why not?

LIZ: Without being a nun or anything I have sort of constructed a persona that doesn't really leave room for blow job jokes.

JOHN: The ferret joke isn't a blow job joke. It's a subversive exploration of the prejudices of its audience.

LIZ: Is it.

MARK: It's a beautiful snowflake.

JOHN: It feints with one overextended comic situation then surprises the listener with a different joke about chauvinist conceptions of women. And in the laughter or the silence it prompts in the listener, which is more genuine and honest thanks to the element of surprise that comes by way of building up the first dummy joke, it invites said listener to learn something about themselves and their own preconceptions.

LIZ: It's not, it's a blowjob joke. You're a tosser, John, but I like you for trying to talk your way out. Should you be drinking this early?

JOHN: No.

LIZ: You will anyway?

JOHN: Yup.

LIZ: I tell him every week but I don't think he believes in liver failure, he thinks it's like the tooth fairy or the female orgasm.

JOHN: I always start with a Holsten Pils about now. Then six or eight of those and then a bit of rosé, maybe a bottle of rosé for the afternoon, then VATs for the evening.

LIZ: VATs?

MARK: Vodka and tonic.

LIZ: Christ, John.

JOHN: It's a lot, isn't it.

LIZ: It's quite a lot. How many vodka and tonics you drink?

JOHN: Sometimes six. Sometimes sixteen.

MARK: I suppose you're a big enough bloke like.

LIZ: You shouldn't do that to yourself.

JOHN: I can hold it. You should stick around some time, you'll find I become quite talkative.

LIZ: I find you quite talkative enough.

MARK: Do you need so much, to feel it then?

JOHN: No, not really. It just helps, is all.

LIZ: How?

JOHN: Well I think there's some comfort in being able to put your finger on precisely what your problem is, you know?

Get your feelings into boxes. If I was just existentially mournful that'd be awful, but because I've got a drinking problem...

LIZ: You've arranged yourself a drinking problem so you can have something concrete to feel depressed about?

JOHN: Exactly. No, I just like a drink really. And it's all free for me, isn't it. At the point of delivery. My little alcoholic NHS in there.

LIZ: Why do you think you're depressed?

JOHN: My wife left me.

LIZ: Oh John.

JOHN: What?

LIZ: You tell such terrible –

JOHN: No, she –

LIZ: Seriously?

JOHN: Yeah.

LIZ: Is he joking?

MARK: Erm –

LIZ: John, I'm so sorry.

JOHN: Nearly a year ago now.

LIZ: Oh fuck. That's why I never see her around any more?

JOHN: That'd probably be it.

LIZ: I thought she must have lie-ins on Sundays or something.

JOHN: No. Not here anyway. Possibly she has lie-ins in Marlborough with her new antique dealing boyfriend.

LIZ: A year?

JOHN: Yeah, been a while now. It's all over really, bar the attention-seeking suicide attempt. Divorce papers an' everythin'. Scrawl on the line. I've written the first fifty thousand words of an agony memoir about it.

LIZ: I've come here every month for two years and you've never said anything.

JOHN: Well it's not something you bring up, is it, really. And you never come in the pub, they all have a laugh about it in there, but you have your drink out here, and I'm not gonna bring you a lemonade and tell you a thing like that. My wife left me. Sounds like an awful chatup line. You might think I was trying it on!

LIZ: I just feel so awful.

JOHN: I bet you do. I've been on the market for a year, you haven't been buyin'. Not that I'd charge, not for you anyway.

LIZ: Oh, John.

JOHN: What? What?

Silence.

MARK: You must get proper fuckin' hangovers drinking that much, right John?

JOHN: I think I'm always just a bit pissed. Specially now. What with. It was already happening before she left, that was how I knew she wasn't making it up. She said something about me and the drink when she left. No, that's unfair. She was clearer than that, I'm being unfair. She said I wasn't the man she'd married any more, and I hadn't been for a long time, and this wasn't the life she'd thought we'd have, and it never had been. And she said she'd turned fifty and it'd made her think, and if she didn't do something with her life now, she'd never be able to live with herself. Cos when the day came that her legs stopped working all she'd have to entertain herself with would be this, us, and

33

it wasn't enough for her. And she said she'd decided she was never going to do anything living with me. Then she told me I drank too much. Then she told me she was sorry. Then she told me I ought to look after myself. Then she left. I had to look at myself and say I suppose you haven't been happy for a long time either. Anyway.

MARK: Fuck mate.

JOHN: Yeah.

LIZ: That's so beautiful.

JOHN: What?

LIZ: I mean it's sad. Beautiful and sad. Same thing.

JOHN: That's a weird little insight into your head right there.

LIZ: Is it? Don't you think the way things sort of just, happen to people, you know?

MARK: You getting a decent send off?

JOHN: Not really. People are keeping away.

MARK: Why?

LIZ: Where are you going?

JOHN: Away. I've sold up.

LIZ: What?

JOHN: My soon to be ex-wife wanted her half of everything. Which is her right, and which she's more than earned, I reckon. So I had to sell up. No money for buying her out of the pub.

LIZ: Fuck.

JOHN: It's all right.

LIZ: No, fuck. Are you all right?

JOHN: Course.

LIZ: Today?

JOHN: I know.

MARK: Why hasn't anyone been round to say goodbye?

JOHN: I don't know mate, do I. I only know they haven't come. I like to think of it as a reminder. Any time I've thought I was anything more than a service to people I've been fooling myself. All I am and ever have been is a supplier of alcoholic products. Which is good for me in a way, keeps me grounded. People don't feel emotional connections to pubs, not really. They say they do, but. They're places to pass through, places to drink in. Or if people do feel emotional connections, it's nothing to do with me. The pub was standing long before I was standing in it, it'll be here long after I'm gone, I'm not really important to the operation, am I. I just lived here for a little while. What matters is the people who drink here, not the people who run it.

LIZ: There are people who'd say you're the life and soul of the place.

JOHN: You might say that. I couldn't possibly comment. But no one's dropped in to say goodbye, so I think you're in a minority.

LIZ: God.

JOHN: I think maybe once you know something's closing it starts to look sick. People maybe steer clear of a place once its notice is posted, in case they catch something. Catch closing time, sort of thing. And apart from anything else I think people are boycotting because I'm selling to the man.

LIZ: No.

MARK: What man?

JOHN: You know.

MARK: No.

LIZ: The / man the man.

JOHN: You know, the man! Don't you say that? Maybe
that's gone out of fashion. Christ I feel old talking to you.
Look, this pub's never been part of a chain before, has
it. Obviously. Nothing's ever been part of a chain round
here. And I won't feel guilty, cos there just aren't people
looking to buy pubs anywhere, and if you have to sell you
have to sell to who's buying, but I do feel ashamed in a
way. Letting a chain in here. Because a pub's a business,
sure, you have to make money, you have to pay your bills,
but it's supposed to be more than that isn't it. It's much
more than that. You have responsibilities. To the soul of a
place. Because there is such a thing as society. It happens
here, I see it every evening. And here I am monetising
conviviality.

MARK: I wouldn't beat yourself up mate. It'll still be selling the
same drinks, won't it.

LIZ: And no one's going to blame you if you didn't have a
choice.

JOHN: It's about sameness, though, isn't it. People like us,
we're supposed to live – I don't know. What would you
say? In defiance of cultural homogeny. That's what living
in the country means. We don't just live here, do we, it's a
philosophy, it's an argument we're making.

LIZ: Yes exactly. That's exactly what it is, I've always thought
that. We believe in long walks and cold showers and early
mornings.

JOHN: Well –

MARK: I don't think that's true.

LIZ: No?

MARK: I think that's true if you can afford it. If. Far as I see,
living here means keeping your head above water. Or
fighting to. And failing, and moving to town, and all that

breaking your heart. And no money and damp in the bedroom and taking a third or fourth job just to stay where you are, like, cos you only know this life you were born to, don't you, and you don't want to change it. And no, no one's going to bed at night praying for – I don't know, an All You Can Eat Buffet, but it's not so different from what you do, so I wouldn't feel too bad mate.

LIZ: Sorry.

MARK: What?

LIZ: I'm sorry.

MARK: Right.

LIZ: I didn't mean to upset you.

MARK: I'm not fucking upset.

Silence.

JOHN: I like you Marky Mark. You're like me.

MARK: Am I?

JOHN: We've got things in common, see Liz, him and me.

LIZ: Yeah?

JOHN: We've both lost women we love.

LIZ: Oh –

MARK: Do you think so?

JOHN: What?

MARK: Do you think we're in the same boat there? Fuck's sake. You had the chance to love her. I just had a few years when I used to know a girl who was too good for me. You had the chance to love her. She'll be too good for me for ever now. I'll never have – well I never will have – well. Fuck's sake.

Silence.

JOHN: I'm sorry Mark.

MARK: No, no.

JOHN: No, but I am. I'm being –

MARK: It's all right.

JOHN: You're right. Yeah. I'm sorry. You're right. I didn't have a chance to make her change her mind, though. I had no say in her decision to take away the meaning of my life. Like that. Just like that. I'm gonna go in.

LIZ: Stay a minute.

JOHN: Why?

LIZ: I don't know. I'm just –

JOHN: I need to get to work really.

LIZ: Are you all right? Will you be all right?

JOHN: I'm all right.

LIZ: Maybe I'll drop round later. We could talk some more.

JOHN: What about?

LIZ: I don't know. If you wanted to talk about how you were feeling.

JOHN: Oh, right. That's not really something I go in for to be honest.

LIZ: OK. Well the offer's there.

JOHN: All right. See you later Mark.

MARK: Yeah all right. I'm sorry John. I didn't mean –

JOHN: I know. At least you're talking to me. Since she left no one talks to me about anything any more. Least of all about her. It's like everyone's trying to keep a secret. Trouble is the secret's out. I'm going in. You two gonna be all right?

MARK: Yeah.

JOHN: Liz?

LIZ: Me? Yes I'm fine. I ought to be going, really. Don't want to be late.

JOHN: I suppose you're not going? To the –

MARK: No. Can't, can I.

JOHN: All right. I have to start on lunch.

Exit JOHN.

MARK: What was that all about?

LIZ: What?

MARK: Your little rendezvous.

LIZ: I just think he might want someone to talk to.

MARK: Oh yeah.

LIZ: I just think he might need some help, is all. He's a kind man, you know. Under all that. He's not actually a wanker. I don't think. He always brings me my drink. I think he looks after me, you know.

MARK: Why do you need looking after?

LIZ: No, I don't mean – I don't need that. I don't need anyone to look after me. Is that the funeral you said you couldn't go to?

MARK: Yeah.

LIZ: You did know her then.

MARK: Yeah.

LIZ: Oh. I'm sorry. I hope I didn't say anything –

MARK: No you're all right.

LIZ: Sometimes I talk too much.

MARK: It's because of the centenary, innit.

LIZ: What?

MARK: That's why there's been a rush to get the memorial done. We're having events like everywhere else. Hundred years on sort of thing. Boo hoo. So the council want it fixed quick as poss cos it's supposed to be part of all the events, see? Something to march past. Trouble is, what maybe looks like a sensible decision at council level, the war memorial's fallen down, let's get it back up again sharpish, always looks a bit different to the people on the ground, you're right. What looks efficient on a meeting agenda looks sort of fucking tasteless when she gets driven past the road works, that's true. And the worst of it is that out here, what starts as a council policy always ends up as a local taking a day's work doing something he wishes he didn't have to, cos he doesn't know how else he's going to pay his rent. So yeah, I know quite a lot about the war memorial getting fixed. It's me that's doing it.

LIZ: Oh.

MARK: I don't want to. She was my best friend. I felt that anyway. She had a lot of friends, but she was *my* best friend. We lived next to each other. Grew up together. But I have to take the work, see. Round here there's little enough before you start turning stuff down on principle. From the fuckin' council an all. You don't wanna be on their blacklist.

LIZ: I'm so sorry.

MARK: I feel so sad about it. Cos she used to let me hold her hand, you know? And I can still feel what that felt like. You know? Yeah.

LIZ: I really didn't mean to be rude. I feel awful.

MARK: You weren't rude. I'm fuckin' furious about it. But I've been a motorway repairman and slept five nights a week in my cab by the side of the road, I've chipped the mortar off bricks while the snow was falling. You do the work, that's all, you do the work there is and pay the rent and pay the rent. There's no say in it. You have to take your work where you can find it. You ought to go, you know. It won't be long before people start arriving. Fuckin' flowers everywhere I suppose, all round the church.

LIZ: Yes. Flowers everywhere. I don't want to leave you like this.

MARK: Like what?

LIZ: You know. I don't know. Sad.

MARK: I don't really think there's anything you can say that's going to do much about that.

LIZ: Right. No. Of course. Well perhaps I'll –

MARK: He's all right you know, John. If you were looking for a character reference. He's all right.

LIZ: It's nothing like that. I just thought he might need a friend, OK?

MARK: All right. Just saying. Nice to meet you.

LIZ: And you. Perhaps I'll see you later.

MARK: Well you'll know where to find me. I'll be putting the memorial back up.

TWO

JOHN is sitting on the bench, a crown on his head, a pewter tankard in his hands. He sits. He looks into the tankard. It's got a glass bottom, and he waves his hand under it then sits up and looks out as if it's a telescope. He cries. Enter LIZ.

JOHN: *(Sings.)* And it's no, nay, never, no nay never no more, and I'll play the wild rover, no never, no more.

LIZ: John?

JOHN: Oh. Sorry. I was –

LIZ: What's the matter?

She sits by him.

JOHN: They all turned up.

LIZ: Who?

JOHN: For the wake of course, they were having the wake here. The whole village. And then –

LIZ: What?

JOHN: Bill Owen, do you know Bill? Oldest buffer here. Father of the village, if you will. Or he likes to act like he is. Lives along in one of the cottages, he's been there since about forty-eight, he's gone ninety. You might not know him, he doesn't go to church. Bill stands up and the place falls silent. The whole village is looking at him. And he says we all know today is a sad day, today is Lucy's day, but there's someone else who's leaving us this evening, and the number of times I've seen Lucy drunk in here I don't think she'd want to let it pass without comment. And he raises a toast to me. To the rest of my life. And the boys get out this cava and spray it all over me, and stick this fucking crown on my head, and say they reckon Lucy would have wanted to join in with that and all. Then Bill gives me this tankard, look. For a present. Look. 'To John, from his friends in the village.' And I just cried. I couldn't help it. I didn't know what to say. I didn't say anything.

LIZ: That's lovely. I think that's lovely.

JOHN: I thought they were keeping away. To show what they thought about things.

LIZ: Of course they weren't keeping away. You will have been loved by people here John, you know all that stuff you were spouting this morning was bollocks. You will have been loved.

JOHN: I thought I'd let them down, is all.

LIZ: You haven't done anything like that. You've done what you must. That's all right. People understand that. *(JOHN cries.)* Hey, hey. Don't cry. OK. Come here. Don't cry. Come on. *(A silence while JOHN recovers himself.)* Well. It must have been a funny note to strike at a wake.

JOHN: I suppose so. I might have one more drink, d'you want one?

LIZ: Not for me, thanks, no.

JOHN: Fair enough. *(He starts looking for a bottle.)* It felt sort of good, though, really. When you thought about things. To raise a glass to something. Because she was lovely, you know? Did you know her?

LIZ: No.

JOHN: I'd have thought she was in your choir. She was a good singer.

LIZ: We don't have a choir, John. Shows how often you go to church.

JOHN: Last time I went there was a choir.

LIZ: That was a concert. I was sitting in front of you, that was some students singing *Acis and Galatea*, that wasn't a choir.

JOHN: I don't know the difference really. It's all singing, innit. Anyway it didn't seem so wrong this afternoon. Her mum and dad were both there, I think they were happy when Bill stood up. Take the attention away, you know? Everyone looking at them and no one knowing what to say. It's such a sad thing, but she was lovely, so it felt sort of good to smile about something.

LIZ: To be a bit happy.

JOHN: Only because she always seemed happy.

LIZ: I know.

JOHN: When you're the bright one or the beautiful one in a place as small as this it stands out, you know? You matter to everyone. In towns, even if you're a genius, you're only ever really a drop in the ocean. We were all proud of her here. Even me, even us outsiders.

LIZ: You weren't an outsider, you were the life and soul of the place.

JOHN: For a little while, yeah.

He has found several beer bottles, but all of them are empty.

JOHN: Oh, fuck. I thought I'd brought enough to last me a while.

He blows on one to make the empty bottle noise.

LIZ: How long have you been out here?

JOHN: Dunno. A while. That's probably why – yeah, right. I'm so fucking hot, you know?

LIZ: Oh John.

JOHN: Sweating like a fat lad.

He blows on two of the other bottles.

LIZ: Look at you.

JOHN: This one isn't finished though.

LIZ: Don't drink it John.

JOHN: What?

LIZ: You've had enough, haven't you.

JOHN: Have I?

LIZ: I think you've had enough.

JOHN: Right. OK. I see.

He puts the bottle down.

JOHN: Don't go calling me a fuckin' alkie, yeah?

LIZ: I'm not, I promise.

JOHN: Cos people get shocked with how much I drink, but I'm all right, you know? I drink two litres of water at bedtime. My kidneys are fine. I got em checked. I don't get the shakes. I can handle my drink.

LIZ: All right.

JOHN: And if you're thinking this is the classic aggressive behaviour of the alcoholic in denial, you can fuck yourself an all, yeah?

He starts taking his shirt off.

LIZ: Do you need to undress now, John?

JOHN: Nah, it's fine. Hot, that's all. You're making a face like it's not fine.

LIZ: I just think we were talking, and now you're taking your clothes off, really.

JOHN: All right, it's all right. Don't worry about it.

He takes off his shirt. He is wearing a t shirt underneath.

JOHN: STELLA!!!

LIZ laughs.

JOHN: Good right? I'm a dead ringer aren't I.

LIZ: For the later Marlon Brando, maybe.

JOHN: Look at this.

He grabs the umbrella for the picnic table and hoists the shirt atop as a flag.

LIZ: What are you doing?

JOHN: Hang on.

LIZ: Be careful.

JOHN: Who are you, my Mum? Look at that!

LIZ: What is it?

JOHN: Well it's a flag, innit. Jolly Roger.

LIZ: It doesn't have a skull and cross bones.

JOHN: No. Not the Jolly Roger then. I suppose we'll just have to do all the rogering ourselves, boom boom!

LIZ: Funny.

JOHN: You know me. Always ready with a one liner. I'd never have believed my father was stealing from his job as a road mender, but I went round his flat the other day and the signs are all there. Boom boom!

LIZ: You're like, half Bruce Forsyth and half Basil Brush, what's happened to you?

JOHN: My brother's addicted to brake fluid, but he says he can stop at any time.

LIZ laughs.

JOHN: This cafe had a sign in the window advertising breakfast at any time, so I went in and asked for French toast during the Renaissance.

LIZ laughs again.

JOHN: I like your laugh.

LIZ: Thank you.

JOHN: I'm pleased you liked my jokes.

LIZ: I sort of felt carpet bombed into submission.

JOHN: I think they call it clusterfucking.

LIZ: Sounds exhausting.

JOHN: Boom boom. Christ, I'm out of breath. Strenuous brilliance, that's what tires me out.

LIZ: All right?

JOHN: Yeah, yeah.

LIZ: So you're actually selling tonight then are you? This is actually it, your last evening? And the man's turning up for the keys tomorrow morning?

JOHN: That's it.

LIZ: God.

JOHN: Weird, innit.

LIZ: I'm so gutted.

JOHN: Why?

LIZ: I don't know. I'm just sad.

JOHN: Gonna miss me?

LIZ: Oh, John.

JOHN: Sad for me you mean.

LIZ: For you, but. I don't know. I've felt like we were getting to know each other, you know? In the time I've been coming here. And I've enjoyed how that's been taking its time, cos I thought we were going to be doing this for years, I thought there was lots of time to, to take. I thought there was loads of chat to look forward to. But you're off.

JOHN: Right. I suppose.

LIZ: You'll definitely go?

JOHN: Yeah.

LIZ: D'you know where yet?

JOHN: No.

LIZ: Mm.

JOHN: What?

LIZ: Could you not stay here? And still be part of it?

JOHN: In the village?

LIZ: Yeah.

JOHN: I don't think I could go and pay for my drinks in there. And what would I do for work anyway? All fucking horrible jobs everyone does round here to make ends meet.

LIZ: That's what drags me out here on a Sunday.

JOHN: How d'you mean?

LIZ: No other jobs. Nowhere any nearer home I can get the gig playing the organ. I'm not any great shakes at it, to be honest, see, so all the bigger places nearer by, nearer my home, they don't want me. Two hours I drive to play here, cos it's the only place that'll have me. It's a crappy little organ. I think they might have scrapped it by now if I didn't keep turning up. So I suppose in a way I keep the habit up for the whole place, singing with an organ, I mean. Which I think is nice.

JOHN: I'm sure everyone appreciates it.

LIZ: Labour of love you know. Twenty quid in petrol money's all they can give.

JOHN: How much does the petrol cost for the drive?

LIZ: Twenty-five quid.

JOHN: That's good. That's very neat.

LIZ: Yeah, I know.

JOHN: Bit colder only wearing a vest.

LIZ: I bet. So this is your last night.

JOHN: Actually last night was my last night really. I think on the forms it says ownership transfers at closing time. I don't even know if I'm allowed to sleep here. I'm going to. Bloke who's having it off me only works nine to five, he won't get here till the morning. And I'll spend tomorrow moving out, there hasn't been time yet. They understand all that. They know it's weird. So I have one more night in there.

LIZ: What will you do with it?

JOHN: I dunno. Probably cry into this funny little tankard.

LIZ: Well that sounds fun.

JOHN: Not to be missed. Why do you do it? The organ playing. If you don't mind me asking.

LIZ: Well it's fun isn't it. And it's only once a month, with the way the services work out.

JOHN: No, but why do you actually do it?

LIZ: What do you mean?

JOHN: Why this and not watercolour painting? Or dogging or whatever.

LIZ: I guess because I believe in it.

JOHN: In God?

LIZ: No, you don't have to believe in God to be an Anglican. That's the whole point. The right to have an equivocal relationship with everything, that's the point. I mean the ritual. And the songs. Some of them are really good songs. It's what we're all brought up with, isn't it. It's where we're all from. I think you have to pay some heed to that. Or someone does. Or I do, anyway.

JOHN: I'm sure people are grateful that you do.

LIZ: I'm sure they're not, I'm sure it never crosses their mind. But if – well imagine that who we are is the sum total of everything that's ever happened to us, right?

JOHN: Right.

LIZ: Well if that's true, if that was true, then I think old ceremonies must be important, because of that. And the church. The church is big you know? Big thing. It's part of the reason for almost everything that's happened, isn't it. Cos everyone ever like, used to read the Bible. All the time. So it's in us, isn't it. Part of. Even the Beatles went to Sunday school, you know?

JOHN: Sure.

LIZ: And people say the church doesn't matter any more. And I think those people can sod off, to be honest, because it makes me so angry to hear someone dismiss another person's culture. And it's bollocks and all. Because it's still who we are, even if we ignore it. And I'm not saying it's a good thing or a bad thing, it's just a fact, it's who we are.

JOHN: As long as you don't think it's an unbridled joy, I can go along with that.

LIZ: No, no. It does terrible bloody damage, the church. But you fix things by getting to the cause, not burying it. And now Rowan Williams tells me we live in a post-Christian society and I think, hang on a minute. Because that's my culture you're attacking, and seeing as you were running the fucking joint a year ago it really ought to be yours to defend as well. And who the hell are all the bishops sitting unelected in the Lords if we live in a post-Christian culture anyway? It's not the truth because look what the Queen's in charge of. He's probably just being paid to run the thing down cos someone wants to buy it.

JOHN: What's your favourite hymn then?

LIZ: What?

JOHN: Go on, you must have a favourite.

LIZ: No!

JOHN: Any hymn.

LIZ: *Praise my Soul The King of Heaven* then, I like that. Oh no, *Abide With Me*. *Abide With Me*. Played that this afternoon. They're by the same guy you know.

JOHN: Yeah?

LIZ: Henry Francis Lyte. Isn't that a lovely name? Actually there's a beautiful story about *Abide With Me*.

JOHN: Go on.

LIZ: Well Lyte was the curate of All Saints Church in Brixham, in Devon. By the sea. And he'd got ill, right? TB. And it was decided he should move to Italy. For his health, they used to think that helped, the climate and whatever. And after he preached for the last time in his church, he'd been there for twenty-seven years, he preached for the last time, and when he was done he went down to the sea. It's like Matthew Arnold, it's like *Dover Beach*. Ah love, let us be true to one another, you know? And while he was on the beach, he had this moment of, I don't know, this inspiration. And he wrote *Abide With Me*. And two weeks later he was dead.

JOHN: No way.

LIZ: Died in Nice on the way down to Italy. But the lovely thing, right, the lovely thing is that you can go down to Brixham and at eight every evening when the light's going out of the sky, in summer anyway, it's dark in the winter of course, but at the same time every evening they play the tune on the church bells. Isn't that lovely?

JOHN: That's lovely. Yeah. Have you been then?

LIZ: No, I just heard about it from a teacher in Salisbury I knew. I wanna go. I just haven't got round to it yet. They did it at the funeral, *Abide With Me*. That was one of the hymns.

JOHN: Oh yeah?

LIZ: Actually I don't like *Abide With Me* best.

JOHN: No?

LIZ: No. If I have to pick one, if I have to pick one it has to be *Dear Lord and Father of Mankind*.

JOHN: That's a good one.

LIZ: You know it?

JOHN sings the first verse of 'Dear Lord and Father of Mankind', and LIZ joins in and sings it with him.

LIZ: Isn't that lovely?

JOHN: Yeah, that's a good one. You know your organ playing?

LIZ: What?

JOHN: Your organ playing.

LIZ: What about it?

JOHN: Well –

LIZ: Go on.

JOHN: Well sometimes I think when I hear people talking a lot, that what they're actually trying to do is not say what's really on their mind. What's actually getting to them.

LIZ: Oh.

JOHN: I was listening to you. Been listening. 'Bout keeping cultures alive or whatever. And I just don't buy it, really. I don't think people act out of such – cos I think you're not happy, Liz, put simply. That's what I think. And I don't think anything happens that isn't about feeling love or lack of love for another person, which might just be me, but that's what I think, so all the time I've been listening to you talk I've been getting this picture. Of a man you don't know any more you wish you still knew. I believe in that much more as an explanation for who you are than the one you've just given me. You mustn't mind me saying this. It's my last day, I want to be honest with you.

LIZ: Right.

JOHN: Am I wrong?

LIZ: You're telling your own story, John, not mine, that's all.

JOHN: My assessment of you –

LIZ: Go on.

JOHN: My assessment of you has always basically been that you're someone who needs to get laid.

LIZ: Excuse me?

JOHN: Don't you think? I think there's a sexual element in everything, I think that's what it is. I think everything is sex.

LIZ: That's very definitely your story, not mine.

JOHN: Maybe. But that's how I see you.

LIZ: Well you can fuck off then John.

JOHN: What?

LIZ: You div.

JOHN: All I'm / trying to say –

LIZ: I was being nice. I was trying to distract you, that's all. From how you were feeling, and you can fuck off do I need to get laid. Of course I need to get laid, don't we all, that's not who I bloody am!

JOHN: Right.

LIZ: God's sake!

JOHN: Sorry.

LIZ: Don't bother, all right? Fuck's sake.

JOHN: I'm sorry. All I was trying to say was that I wanted to kiss you.

LIZ: Right. I see. I'm going to go now.

JOHN: Oh. / You don't –

LIZ: I was only trying to be nice. I suppose you're unstable because of your wife.

JOHN: I'm not –

LIZ: You're such an idiot. You're such a fucking idiot. I've so liked talking to you, out here, our little chats, I've always looked forward to them. Never expecting anything to – come of it, that was what was so – because you had a wife, you were someone I could just talk to, you were finally someone to talk to. But you don't have a wife. Do you. And here I am. And I thought – I've always thought. All you had to do was not fuck it up, John, because I've thought the world of you all the time I've been driving out here. And now you've fucked it up. There you go. That's that. I'm going to go. I'm going to go. Good luck in the future John, all right? Whatever you do with it. Have a good life.

JOHN: Liz.

LIZ: I have to go. Good bye. I – good bye.

JOHN: Liz –

LIZ exits. JOHN sits alone. He hears someone coming, and stops, embarrassed.

Enter MARK.

MARK: All right.

JOHN: All right.

MARK puts his tool kit down.

JOHN: You done then?

Silence.

MARK: How was the –?

MARK sits.

MARK: Was that that funny woman from the church?

JOHN: Leave it will you Mark? Let it remain as a beautiful snowflake.

THREE

MARK is wearing a suit. He has a fag. Enter LIZ, also dressed smartly.

LIZ: I know you, don't I?

MARK: Scuse me?

LIZ: Haven't we met before?

MARK: Last year. I –

LIZ: That's it.

MARK: You're the organist.

LIZ: That's me. Liz.

MARK: Mark.

LIZ: Yes. Hello again Mark. Isn't it a beautiful day?

MARK: Yeah.

LIZ: This is a lovely village in the sun.

MARK: Yeah.

LIZ: I'm excited, seeing it on a Saturday. I don't usually come up here Saturdays, but there's a wedding.

MARK: Yeah.

LIZ: It's your wedding?

MARK: Yeah.

LIZ: Congratulations! That's lovely. That's so lovely. How are you feeling?

MARK: Yeah. I mean. It's pretty –

LIZ: It's the same for everyone, don't worry. I've done a lot of weddings. All the grooms I see, it's a big day.

MARK: Yeah.

LIZ: A happy day, but you get scared as well.

MARK: Exactly.

LIZ: Because in theory, this is the last person you'll ever shag, isn't it. And I know for a man that's quite –

MARK: I'm not worried about that.

LIZ: No? Well that's good then.

MARK: Yeah.

LIZ: Just the bloody magnitude of it.

MARK: Loads of things. I, erm. Actually. I don't know whether I can do it, actually.

LIZ: How d'you mean?

MARK: I just don't know – I don't know if I can do it'.

LIZ: Oh right.

MARK: I just thought I'd hide for a minute, you know, just –

LIZ: Right. That's why you're –

MARK: No one really comes round here, yeah. It's a bit like. Horrible. I don't know –

LIZ: Do you want me to / leave you alone?

MARK: No, no, it might be good to have someone to – I'm just scared, you know? Really – it's so weird like. And I can't talk to any of my mates, I can't.

LIZ: What's up?

MARK: It feels quite fast, you know? It feels quite fast. And I don't want to make a mistake. Cos I'd hurt her, if I was, and I couldn't bear it, you know? Cos she's amazing. I love her, you know? Only it feels quite fast.

LIZ: When did you meet?

MARK: Years back. School, like. She was below me in school. I sort of knew her, not properly but. But we started seeing each other like, nine months ago.

LIZ: OK. That's not so fast if everything's wonderful?

MARK: Yeah, and everything is, everything is wonderful. But I feel so lucky, you know? I can't believe my luck, that someone wanted me. So I feel like I'm pushing my luck. This. And I didn't think this would ever, ever happen to me, and it's now it's fucking happening today, and you're like – fuck.

LIZ: Right, yeah.

MARK: So that's it really.

LIZ: Right. What are you gonna do?

MARK: I dunno. My head's like.

LIZ: Yeah.

MARK: I keep thinking about all the things I thought I'd have done before I got married.

LIZ: Oh yeah?

MARK: Not big things. I don't mind not having done them, even. I never had a proper plan or. Just – you know. I don't think I ever thought it was the sort of thing that. It's so real, isn't it.

LIZ: What did you want to do? Before you got married, I mean.

MARK: Well nothing big or anything. I haven't been to Wembley yet.

LIZ: Wembley's quite big.

MARK: I wanted to have filled the bookshelf in my room.

LIZ: What with?

MARK: Books.

LIZ: Yeah, what books?

MARK: Oh, anything really. I'm not picky. Just books I'd read. Anything I could get in Sue Ryder. There's better stuff in charity shops than you'd think.

LIZ: And what else did you plan to have done?

MARK: I was going to see the world.

LIZ: But you haven't?

MARK: Not really. I had a bit of a disastrous attempt.

LIZ: Oh yes?

MARK: Yeah. I was going with a friend, round the world, you know, I was going to go travelling. This was years ago, this was when I was a teenager. Really looking forward to it. But they changed their mind about going with me, went round the world with someone else, my friend did.

LIZ: Nice.

MARK: Yeah. So I went on my own. And I spent about a week in India and it was just horrible, really, so I came home.

LIZ: Oh.

MARK: Yeah.

LIZ: And you'd planned to stay out longer?

MARK: Like six months, yeah.

LIZ: Well six months is a lot of time to spend on your own.

MARK: Yeah. I sometimes wish I'd stayed out there.

LIZ: Yeah?

MARK: Well I didn't get any refunds so it cost the same going for a week as it would have done going for half a year.

More or less. What with the extra flights and all. And I'd
quit my job and they wouldn't give it back so –

LIZ: That's a shame.

MARK: And I did – I felt I'd failed a bit. And I do feel like
I haven't lived now, now that I'm settling down here
properly. Haven't really tested myself or anything.

LIZ: What was so horrible about India, do you mind me asking?

MARK: Oh, it's hard to explain. I saw a dog tear a cat in two.

LIZ: Right.

MARK: Creep up on it and shake it till it came apart. I saw this
child, this naked child squatting down to take a shit on a
big pile of other people's shit, and these school children
passing just spat at it. And the little kid looked so ashamed.

LIZ: God.

MARK: And the beggars. Guys with their eyes gouged out, you
know? And sewed back up. These little girls would come
up and ask me to buy them powdered milk for their baby
brothers, then take you in a shop and you'd get charged
like twenty quid for a packet. And I knew it was a stitch up
but I just had to do it cos when you go out at night, there
are literally hundreds of people just lying down in the road
to sleep. You know?

LIZ: That's awful.

MARK: I spent about three hundred quid on powdered milk,
just in the one week. Thought I deserved it. I just thought,
you cunt. Coming over here like it's an adventure. When
it's these people's lives. You don't know a fucking thing
about anything. You deserve to be taken for all you've got.
That was my attempt at widening my horizons. That was
that. I thought it was so disrespectful to be there like I was.
Without contributing anything. Just staring at everything.
So all the money I didn't spend on powdered milk I took
into Thomas Cook, this beautiful Thomas Cook with

beautiful air conditioning, and I spent all the money I had on a plane ticket home.

LIZ: You really didn't like it then.

MARK: I hated myself for being there. I was an extra in a Bollywood movie. But yeah. That was that, anyway. Yeah.

LIZ: And this friend who didn't go with you, that was your friend who died, was it?

MARK: What?

LIZ: I just thought you might be thinking of her, today. If she meant things to you.

MARK: Right. Yeah. God, do you remember that?

LIZ: Of course.

MARK: Right, yeah, of course. Well yeah, I suppose that's why I'm thinking of. It is a bit quick, isn't it.

LIZ: I don't know.

MARK: No?

LIZ: Well it depends on how you feel, doesn't it.

MARK: Yeah. I suppose so.

LIZ: It was a suicide, wasn't it, her death.

MARK: What?

LIZ: I thought it was a suicide.

MARK: No. No one ever said anything like that.

LIZ: Oh, I'm sorry.

MARK: She just hadn't driven her car for a year. She'd had a few drinks and she wasn't used to driving and she was going a bit fast and she lost control.

LIZ: How sad.

MARK: It wasn't a suicide.

LIZ: No, no.

MARK: Did someone tell you that?

LIZ: No! I'm just misremembering. I never quite knew the facts of the thing, and she was a student, wasn't she, and a lot of the time it's students who – and all I remembered was that she drove into the war memorial. I remember that, that phrase. And I'm just getting confused by language, I see it now. Because 'drove' seems like such a deliberate word, doesn't it? But of course it doesn't have to mean she did it deliberately.

MARK: It just means she was driving. She didn't do it on purpose.

LIZ: No. That's good then. I mean, not good, sad. But better than – you know.

MARK: Yeah. Anyway. Yeah.

The sound of singing from the front of the pub. They listen for a moment.

MARK: I never thought anyone would ever actually love me. And I think someone does. And I fucking love them. And I'm so scared of fucking it up because it's all come too soon after – yeah. You know what I mean.

LIZ: Of course. Well maybe you're being sensible. Maybe you're right. Or maybe you just have to suck it and see, you know? People start early at a wedding, don't they! Is the party afterwards here as well?

MARK: We'll end up here in the evening I reckon. We're going to the big house for the meal, like, the lunch. Place on your left when you drive in?

LIZ: There's a wall and a big gate?

MARK: The house is sort of behind a lot of trees, yeah. That's the main place here. And we're both from here, me and my – Rhiannon –

LIZ: 'My wife and I'!

MARK: Yeah. So we hired the lawn and we've got a marquee. They've done us a deal.

LIZ: And the weather's fine, so you've been lucky. Someone's smiling on this one!

MARK: I hope so.

LIZ: So it's a big old stately home, behind the wall?

MARK: Well, sort of. The actual house is only really fifteen years old.

LIZ: Oh?

MARK: There used to be a big house there before. Local MP lived in it. Nice enough bloke. Not sure about his politics. Anyway, one night there was this fire. Someone left a hob on or something, I don't know. And the whole place went up, and sort of collapsed in on itself. And the fire was so strong, so fierce, they never even found the bodies. The people who lived in the house. Whole family gone.

LIZ: God.

MARK: I know. After they'd finished with it as a crime scene, or whatever, the site got sold, and this property developer bought it. He'd made his money building blocks of flats in Bristol, and he wanted a place to live, so he rebuilt the house. Room for room, brick for brick, used the original plans, he lives there now with his family.

LIZ: And does he have anything to do with everyone? Or with the work here, with the farming?

MARK: Farming's all sold off to big outfits years ago. Big operations run all this now.

LIZ: Do they do sheep?

MARK: Some sheep, yeah.

LIZ: I like sheep. Some people say cows are nicer but I think they kill people who walk their dogs. It was all farming I suppose, all this village. Before everyone who lived here was an old age pensioner I mean. Everyone was a farmer.

LIZ: Shame.

MARK: I dunno. The people who lived here were more or less serfs.

LIZ: Yeah?

MARK: The big house paid out wages, but they took plenty back in rents, cos he owned all the cottages. Right? And the wages used to get paid out over the bar in the pub, so plenty got spent straight away in there. And the big house owned the pub as well. So in a way he never really spent any money on the people who worked for him. Just passed a few coins round till they came back into his hands a week later, one way or another.

LIZ: There must be books and books about it. Social history. People writing memoirs. 'Confessions of a shepherd' sort of thing.

MARK: I suppose there are.

LIZ: Do you have those sorts of books on your shelf, do you read about the country?

MARK: A bit. It's more spy novels really.

LIZ: Fair enough. I love a history book, me. The book I always think I'd like to read when I drive up over the chase is a history of road laying.

MARK: A history of road laying?

LIZ: No, it would be interesting! I'd love to know what everyone thought when all this tarmac started happening everywhere. Because that must have been such a shock to the psyche. Of the whole country. All those dirt tracks or whatever getting inked in for ever. It's like. It's like your war memorial isn't it.

MARK: My war memorial?

LIZ: The one you fixed. People live and die in villages like this all the time, don't they, and bit by bit the population of a village will change completely without anyone really noticing it. Like a body's cells are all replaced every seven years, is that right? But write some deaths into stone, you've got this much blunter portrait of a moment in time, you can't help but look at how a place has changed, can you.

MARK: Yeah.

LIZ: Well it's the same with roads for me. Surely for as long as roads were really just places where enough people had walked to make a track there must always have been a suspicion that they were invented, right? Like a dream. That enough people walking in a different direction could change the way a road went. But then you put down tarmac, and things are fixed for ever.

MARK: I suppose that might be an interesting book.

LIZ: I'm full of good ideas, me. I can always think of interesting books I could have written if only I'd been living at the right time. The trouble is we don't seem to be living through anything right now.

MARK: No?

LIZ: No, not really. I just mean it's hard to get things right while they happen to you isn't it. To see, clearly. That's what I think anyway. You're going to be my last gig here, you know.

MARK: Really?

LIZ: I have to stop doing it. Playing here, I mean. The organ. I'm pleased it's you who's getting married, it's nice that it's someone I know.

MARK: I'm gonna go through with it then am I?

LIZ: I was hoping I might be able to slip that in without you noticing.

MARK: Said the bishop to the narcoleptic.

LIZ: *(Laughs.)* You're as bad as John.

MARK: I ought to be, I've got his job now.

LIZ: Have you?

MARK: Well, sort of. I'm the assistant manager.

LIZ: I didn't know that! God have I said anything rude about it? Only I do think the sexual politics of the calendars hanging in the loos are quite problematic, and sometimes I blurt things out.

MARK: No, you're all right.

LIZ: Thank God.

MARK: What's wrong with the calendars in the loos? It's just the local hunt doing *Calendar Girls*, it's all for charity.

LIZ: Yes, but you've had it open on the same month for about a year now, and I had a flick through and it's definitely because the girls from May 2013 have got the nicest arses.

MARK: Oh, yeah, they have. Is that bad?

LIZ: It is a bit bad, I think.

MARK: Sorry.

LIZ: Well, just something to think about maybe.

MARK: How come you're stopping playing the organ? You said I was your last gig.

LIZ: Oh, lots of reasons. The organ's shot, for one thing, and they'll never afford to replace it.

MARK: No?

LIZ: Organs are expensive. And I don't know whether they should be much of a priority these days for churches.

MARK: Why not?

LIZ: I sort of think raising funds to help poor people or the elderly or whatever might be more important, you know? Is this what you want to be talking about, is this –

MARK: All I want to do is not talk about that. Just for a little bit longer.

LIZ: OK.

MARK: So will you tell me something else? Anything else. About why they shouldn't fix the organ, or whatever, I don't care, I'm not really listening, I just don't want to think.

LIZ: Sure. OK. Well, I don't think they ought to renew the organ because you know, music changes as well, you know, and I sometimes think a church trying to fix its organ runs the risk of looking stuck in the past. Because music changes. And God knows, it's my culture, I love organ music, and imagining the history of it, all the people who've sung the same hymns over the years, all the people over history brought together in a way by that, and even a year ago I thought it was all worth saving. I thought it was important it ought to be saved. But the world changes, doesn't it.

MARK: It does.

LIZ: And if people want drum kits in church perhaps they should be allowed them. It seems sad, somehow, but that's just me being stuck in the past, I should think. I'm talking too much about organs. You must need to get back to your people.

MARK: No, they know I wanted a minute.

LIZ: I think what I feel very conscious of is the fact that everything comes to an end, you see. A time always comes when it's time to move on. When I started coming here I was in quite a sad place, actually. Quite a sad bloody place. So I was looking for things to do, so I could drown out my spare time. And these days I feel much better about all that, so I don't think I need all the driving here and back as much.

MARK: What do you do for a living?

LIZ: I teach piano.

Enter JOHN.

JOHN: Hands off cocks, on socks!

LIZ: Oh.

MARK: Fucking hell, hello John!

JOHN: All right mate, how's tricks?

MARK: Good man, yeah. It's so good to see you!

JOHN: Course it is.

MARK: I didn't know whether you'd got your invitation.

JOHN: No?

MARK: You didn't reply to it.

JOHN: No?

MARK: I don't know whether there's a seat for you at lunch.

JOHN: Ah well. 'My bad', as the cool kids say. You'll be able to fit me in?

MARK: I dunno mate, to be honest. It's all like –

JOHN: I'll skip a course and come to the party. Sorry mate. Should have written back. Hello Liz, how are you?

He gives her a kiss on the cheek.

LIZ: Hello John.

JOHN: You look well.

LIZ: Thank you. So do you.

JOHN: Do I? Christ, imagine what I must have looked like when you saw me last. So you're having second thoughts are you?

MARK: What?

JOHN: Everyone knows, mate. Stands to reason. It's your wedding day and you're chain smoking round the back of the pub. Aren't they sweet, the young? They think it's all happening for the first time.

LIZ: Well it is for him.

JOHN: That's true. Mark, I want you to listen to me.

MARK: Right.

LIZ: John –

JOHN: It's all right. Mark. You have never believed you were worth much. But you always have been. You were shit at peeling potatoes when you used to work here, but everyone liked having you around. And you lost someone, very recently. But life goes on, mate. And here's someone standing with their hand out waiting for you. And you have to make a decision.

MARK: Right.

JOHN: Because things don't always happen at the pace we'd choose. So maybe this is all happening a little bit quickly. And it's hard to get your head round. But that's life, isn't it. And I suppose you have to ask yourself this. Do you want to try? Or would you rather never risk anything?

MARK: Right.

JOHN: You see what I mean, don't you.

MARK: Yeah.

JOHN: Well don't be a cunt then.

MARK: OK. Right. Yeah.

JOHN: Probably time to get down the church an all.

MARK: Is it? Oh Christ. I'd better go.

JOHN: Good man. Feel good?

MARK: Yeah. Yeah. I feel good. Yeah. Thanks.

JOHN: Fuck off.

MARK: Thanks Liz.

LIZ: Are you all right?

MARK: Yeah.

LIZ: Are you going to be all right?

MARK: Yeah. Yeah. I feel really good.

MARK exits.

JOHN: Sweet boy, isn't he.

LIZ: He's so frightened.

JOHN: So was I. Were you ever married?

LIZ: Yeah.

JOHN: What happened to your husband?

LIZ: He died.

JOHN: Oh, Liz.

LIZ: Yeah. Congenital cardiomyopathy.

JOHN: Fuck. I'm sorry.

LIZ: Me too. It was years ago now though. I was very scared as well.

JOHN: Yeah. I didn't know Liz, I'm sorry.

LIZ: You don't have anything to apologise for. I ought to get down the church if he's headed that way. It'd be typical me if the bride came up the aisle and I was still puffing my way up the hill. It's nice to see you.

JOHN: I hoped I'd see you.

LIZ: Oh yeah?

JOHN: Yeah.

LIZ: Well. We're lucky then aren't we.

JOHN: Yeah, I guess we are.

LIZ: I'd better make a start.

JOHN: Sure, of course. See you later maybe.

LIZ: OK.

JOHN: Bye then.

LIZ: Bye John. Bye.

LIZ exits.

FOUR

The evening of the wedding. Sound of a good night from the front of the pub. JOHN is sitting with a pint, staring into it. Enter MARK, lighting up.

MARK: So this is where you're hiding.

JOHN: I didn't know you smoked.

MARK: You all right?

JOHN: What?

MARK: Are you all right?

JOHN: Oh, you know me.

MARK: What does that mean?

JOHN: I'm all right.

MARK: All right.

JOHN: Yeah. So have you got my job here, then? Someone told me this is your gaffe now.

MARK: No, erm, assistant manager.

JOHN: Fuck off.

MARK: Yeah, not just a pretty face.

JOHN: What does a pub need an assistant manager for?

MARK: Yeah, yeah. It's all the same work. We just have different titles.

JOHN: I bet you've got a microwave.

MARK: What?

JOHN: I bet you've got a microwave.

MARK: Yeah.

JOHN: There you go. Not all the same, is it. I wouldn't have let one of those through the door. But everything slides under capitalism, dunnit. Anyway. Good show this afternoon.

MARK: Yeah, it was all right, wasn't it.

JOHN: Felt good doing it?

MARK: Fucking amazing actually.

JOHN: Yeah?

MARK: Really like – sure of it. Yeah. Certain. What the fuck is all this? Someone's kicked the hose over. It was probably you.

JOHN: Probably.

The boys in the pub start singing football songs.

JOHN: Listen to that. Piss heads.

MARK: Yeah.

JOHN: Your mates. You know what they say, don't you? By his friends shall you know him.

MARK: Yeah.

JOHN: Not often you get everyone you care about in the same room, is it.

MARK: No, it's cool.

JOHN: Good things, weddings. Break up the slog.

MARK: Yeah.

MARK starts sorting out the hose.

JOHN: Want a hand?

MARK: You're all right.

JOHN: Go on, we can start at different ends. It'll be like *Lady and the Tramp.*

MARK: All right.

JOHN: I'm glad you're working here though, that's good news. Bit of continuity. Nice to know they haven't just shipped in a bunch of Poles from Andover, you know?

MARK: We haven't got any Poles, no.

JOHN: Not that there'd be anything wrong with that, of course.

MARK: We've got a Slovenian girl.

JOHN: Oh yeah?

MARK: She's nice. She's gonna be an interior designer. And we've got two Filipino brothers called Joey and Ken. Well, those aren't their real names. They changed them when they came over to sound more English.

JOHN: What were their names before?

MARK: Joey's name was Irisjim.

JOHN: Yeah, the locals'd laugh at that.

MARK: Ken's funnier though. You'll like Ken's.

JOHN: Why?

MARK: His real name was Edward.

JOHN: That's brilliant.

MARK: Changed it from Edward to Ken to sound more English. They picked the new ones out of *Friends* and *Barbie*.

JOHN: Is that what passes for English culture in the Philippines?

MARK: They might have been spinning me a yarn. They're funny boys. Quicker than me anyway. They're both training as accountants. In Bournemouth.

JOHN: Oh yeah?

MARK: You've done your coils bigger than mine.

JOHN: That's all right isn't it?

MARK: Guess so. Stick it on the table.

JOHN: Don't you want it in the shed?

MARK: They'll water the grass out front in the morning.

JOHN: You water the grass?

MARK: Yeah. It looks nicer.

JOHN: But you water the fucking grass?

MARK: It needs water, dunnit.

JOHN: Things really have changed.

MARK: There's nothing wrong with watering the grass.

JOHN: No, no. I'm sure it's very neat and tidy.

MARK: Yeah.

The boys in the pub are singing pop songs.

JOHN: You were telling me about your Filipino mates.

MARK: Yeah. Well. Nothing really to say about them. They're my mates. Yeah. I've learned a bit of Filipino so I can understand what they're talking about when it's just the three of us, on shift. I wanted to know when they were swearing at me so I asked them to teach me all their swear words and they've only got one. Mangman ikao.

JOHN: What's that mean then?

MARK: Everything, basically. You're a cunt, you're a wanker, you're a fucktard, whatever. Ikao's you are. Ako's I am.

JOHN: Cool.

MARK: I know some other ones too.

JOHN: Go on then.

MARK: Pagod ako. I'm tired. Goutom ako. I'm hungry. Salamat. Thank you. Pashensa. I'm sorry. Bogi ako. I'm handsome. Maganda ikao. She's beautiful.

JOHN: Little Rosetta Stone aren't you.

MARK: I knew some other stuff but I forgot. Keeps me entertained on shift, trying to remember it all.

JOHN: I guess you can't entertain yourself by drinking while you work any more.

MARK: No, there's none of that. But we have a laugh. You've got to have a laugh, haven't you.

JOHN: No you haven't.

MARK: Oh.

JOHN: That's what kids think. Fun. That's not how it goes. I'll tell you how it goes, Mark. You've got to work and then you've got to die.

MARK: Oh.

JOHN: And you've got to get married, of course.

MARK: Yeah. That's quite fun.

JOHN: You wait and see, poor bugger.

MARK: Yeah, maybe.

JOHN: You'll be all right, I reckon. Keep off the drink. Don't forget her birthday. And enjoy tonight. You going on holiday?

MARK: Yeah. Bournemouth.

JOHN: Bournemouth?

MARK: Shit, sorry, no. Brighton.

JOHN: I was gonna fucking say. Christ, Bournemouth. That'd be a short marriage.

MARK: Right.

JOHN: How long have you been working here then?

MARK: 'Bout six months now I think.

JOHN: Yeah? It's so weird to think you're married now.

MARK: Why?

JOHN: You're a little kid.

MARK: Little married kid.

JOHN: Christ.

MARK: Yeah.

JOHN: Where you living now?

MARK: Well, that's the bad news. We're actually living in Andover.

JOHN: Fuck off.

MARK: Nothing we can afford round here.

JOHN: That's a shame, mate, I'm sorry.

MARK: It's not what we'd want, obviously. But you do what you must, don't you.

JOHN: Of course. So you live in Andover and commute out here to work?

MARK: That's it. So how are you, anyway?

JOHN: Pretty good, actually. I contacted a stockbroker I used to serve in here when I left, and he invested the money I got from my half of the pub in futures. And the portfolio's performed pretty well, and I'm actually a millionaire now.

MARK: Seriously?

JOHN: No, course not. But I'm all right. I haven't really decided what to do with the rest of my miserable life, yet, mind.

MARK: Still?

JOHN: It's only been a year.

MARK: Yeah. All the same, John. Gotta enjoy it while it lasts, haven't you.

JOHN: I've had bits and bobs of fun, don't worry. I've got all the money I got for her to spend, haven't I. Did a bit of travelling. The mountains of Nepal.

MARK: What was that like?

JOHN: It was all right. Mountains were nice. I'm not convinced about travelling though.

MARK: No?

JOHN: I don't know why all these eighteen year olds do it. The odd nice view, but you're basically always just looking for things to do, you know?

MARK: Oh yeah?

JOHN: Yeah. Cos there's no work, and there's only so many hours a day you can spend being fascinated by how foreign everything is. Specially at my age, when your ankles swell up. Still, kids like it don't they.

MARK: They do.

JOHN: If I had a kid I'd tell him not to bother. You get more out of getting on with something, I think, that's what I wish I could do. I just can't think of anything to get on with.

MARK: That's cos you're sad, you not liking travelling.

JOHN: Yeah?

MARK: A traveller, on his journey, changes only his skies and not his self.

JOHN: Where's that from?

MARK: Can't remember. Some book I read in the loo. Someone's Facebook cover photo.

JOHN: You kept up the reading?

MARK: There isn't time really.

JOHN: Can I ask you something?

MARK: Go on.

JOHN: I always thought you'd get out of here one day. What with all your books. Bright bloke that you are. Cos there's not much here for you, is there, unless you always wanted to be an assistant manager.

MARK: Is that a question?

JOHN: Well, are you planning on doing anything, is all I meant? Have you got a plan?

MARK: I'm making one.

JOHN: Right. Yeah.

MARK: One foot in front of the other.

JOHN: Yeah. Can I ask you something else?

MARK: Don't ask me about her, John, will you?

JOHN: I just / wondered how you were about –

MARK: It's all in the past, yeah? It's all something I'm moving on from.

JOHN: Probably a good thing. Probably good to keep trucking on.

MARK: Yeah.

JOHN: And you've found someone you love.

MARK: Yeah, I have. And I married her. Cos I didn't see the point in living in the past John, in dreaming. Cos the brave thing people do is get on with it, you know? So I married her. And when I needed a job I found a job.

JOHN: And heaven knows you're miserable now.

They laugh.

JOHN: Isn't it funny how time just seems to happen to you? And you never really seem to do anything except go along with it.

MARK: Oh, there are deliberate decisions you make along the way. I took up smoking.

JOHN: Your Dad'd be proud.

MARK: Yeah.

JOHN: I stopped drinking.

MARK: Did you?

JOHN: No. But I drink much less cos I can't get it at cost any more.

MARK: I bet. Do you wanna come and see in the kitchen, everything we've cocked up since you left?

JOHN laughs.

MARK: What?

JOHN: I don't think so.

MARK: No? Fair enough.

JOHN: I had my life in there, you know? I slept in there for fifteen years. This was my life, here.

MARK: OK.

JOHN: Sorry. Nothing to do with you.

MARK: Said the gypsy to the concentration camp commandant.

JOHN: That was one of mine, wasn't it?

MARK: Yeah. No one's very good at jokes round here any more.

JOHN: No?

MARK: I don't know how you came up with all yours.

JOHN: Joke books mate. You didn't think I was making them all up did you?

MARK: Oh. I thought you did.

JOHN: No, read joke books to keep me sane. Hm.

MARK: I'd better go back really.

JOHN: Course.

MARK: It was really good of you to come. Meant a lot to have you there.

JOHN: Wouldn't have missed it.

MARK: You wanna come in with me?

JOHN: In a minute, yeah. Everyone still comes in then do they?

MARK: Yeah. Apart from Bill Owen. You remember Bill?

JOHN: Yeah?

MARK: Dead.

JOHN: Oh yeah.

MARK: Apart from that everyone still comes in.

JOHN: I hoped they'd stay away once I left. Not seriously. Not actually. I do know it's their pub. I just hoped a bit they might want to stick it to the man.

MARK: I don't think they think of a pint as a political act.

JOHN: Fair enough.

MARK: You'll be all right, yeah, John? You'll find something you want to do soon.

JOHN: Thanks mate. Oh, I meant to ask.

MARK: Yeah?

JOHN: Liz. The organist. Have you seen her around? I wanted to talk to her.

MARK: I think she's gone actually.

JOHN: Oh.

MARK: She said she had to head home.

JOHN: Oh.

MARK: Said she wouldn't have a drink cos she didn't like drinking and driving.

JOHN: Oh. Would you know where I could look her up, by any chance?

MARK: The church'll have her number?

JOHN: Yeah. Good thought. The church. She seem all right when you last saw her?

MARK: Yeah, she was all right.

JOHN: Mm. I had it in mind to talk to her, about something. Something. But she's gone has she?

MARK: Yeah, she left after the service.

JOHN: Well. Maybe if she's happy I'll leave it at that. Hey Mark.

MARK: Yeah?

JOHN: I bet the first thing you did when you started was block up that grate. You used to hate that, didn't you.

MARK: No, the fire's still going.

JOHN: Oh yeah?

MARK: Yeah. It's like you said, that's what we're selling, really. Sweat and dogs.

JOHN: Did I say that?

MARK: Don't you remember?

JOHN: I don't remember very much sometimes Mark. I think I fucked my head.

MARK: Don't be silly mate.

JOHN: No, I do, I think I drank myself stupid. Sometimes I don't remember much.

MARK: John.

JOHN: I'm all right. I'm happy today, this is a proper happy fucking day.

MARK: You'll find things to do, John.

JOHN: Yeah.

MARK: I remember a lot of your little sayings. Think of you a lot.

JOHN: Yeah?

MARK: Bit of a mantra that, for me. Sweat and dogs. Bit of a Bible of what I'm up to. You taught me everything I know about market positioning.

JOHN: Well that's some comfort I suppose. I don't suppose you'd know who gives out the jobs round here would you?

MARK: What?

JOHN: In your chain. You know, your – well I was just thinking, they must have other pubs need running, right? You couldn't, like, ask the right person if they need an old landlord anywhere for me, could you?

MARK: I think it's all apply online now.

JOHN: Oh.

MARK: They advertise it online and you upload your CV for central office, yeah.

JOHN: Right.

MARK: I don't really –

JOHN: No, of course, stupid thought. Just. Nah, stupid.

MARK: I can give you the web address? Get it on my phone, hang on. It'll be like / www. –

JOHN: No, you're all right mate, sorry. That's not me. I'm moving on. That's not me. I'm gonna move on.

MARK: You'll be all right.

JOHN: Yeah.

The boys in the pub start singing 'Abide With Me.' JOHN and MARK listen to them.

JOHN: Fuck, I'm a miserable bastard, aren't I. Sorry mate. You got fucking married!

MARK: Yeah!

JOHN: It's amazing, isn't it? You got your life right!

MARK: Yeah. That's a nice way of. Yeah. Day I left school I came here with Lucy. And we drank a bit and we started arguing, cos she wasn't going to leave her boyfriend, she was going out with this older guy and she told me she loved me but. And I started to get upset. Cos I knew even then, I knew it wasn't gonna happen. She was never going travelling with me. And I knew in five years' time we wouldn't know each other any more. And she stood on this bench and made me get up there with her. And she pointed at the big house and the view, and she said look over there. See that? That's the world. That's where we're gonna go. We're gonna do everything. We're gonna have the most brilliant time. And when we get back to England we won't forget each other. Because we'll have shared the whole world, won't we. We're gonna live the best lives ever. We're gonna do everything we want. And I love what I have now. But I'm so glad I had that afternoon. Cos for an afternoon, I believed that. I got to believe that. The lights go down.

END